an eye on * protect * nurse * tend * forgive * care for * give

play * irritate us * weave stories * can relate * s

s giggle * wash behind our ears * give us the world * forgiv

* count to ten * teach * hug and kiss * protect * weave storie

ud * know what's best * tickle and giggle * welcome us hom

an eye on * protect * nurse * tend * forgive * care for * love

play * irritate us * weave stories * can relate * hug and kiss

s giggle * wash behind our ears * give us the world * forgiv

* count to ten * teach * hug and kiss * protect * weave storie

ud * know what's best * tickle and giggle * welcome us hom

an eye on * protect * nurse * tend * forgive * care for * give

play * irritate us * weave stories * can relate * hug and kiss

s giggle * wash behind our ears * give us the world * forgiv

* count to ten * teach * hug and kiss * protect * weave storie

ud * know what's best * tickle and giggle * welcome us hom

an eye on * protect * nurse * tend * forgive * care for * gi

care for * cultivate * attend to * watch over * look after * keep
love * heal * get tough * get all mushy * reach out * inspire
embarrass * give us peace of mind * lend us a hand * make
heal * kick us out * tickle * bathe * welcome us home * listen
deserve the best * scold * feed * give us the world * make us p
care for * cultivate * attend to * watch over * look after * keep
love * heal * get tough * get all mushy * reach out * inspire
embarrass * give us peace of mind * lend us a hand * make
heal * kick us out * tickle * bathe * welcome us home * listen
deserve the best * scold * feed * give us the world * make us p
care for * cultivate * attend to * watch over * look after * keep
love * heal * get tough * get all mushy * reach out * inspire
embarrass * give us peace of mind * lend us a hand * make
heal * kick us out * tickle * bathe * welcome us home * listen
deserve the best * scold * feed * give us the world * make us p
care for * cultivate * attend to * watch over * look after * keep

Mother
IS A VERB

Mina Parker

Conari Press

Mom,

You are the best a kid could ask for. Thanks for all you do. It's what keeps this family running.
Love,
Joshua

mother

Function: *transitive verb*

Inflected Form(s): **moth_ered**; **moth_er_ing** /'m&-[th]&-ri[ng], 'm&[th]-ri[ng]/

1 a : to give birth to **b** : to give rise to : **PRODUCE**

2 : to care for or protect like a mother

Mother. Mom. Ma. Madre. Mama. Mommy.

We don't need a dictionary; for most of us it's the first word we ever know. And besides being the name we call out when we're sick, afraid, or proud of our accomplishments — mother is a verb. Always doing, helping, loving, sharing, and so much more. So here's to mothers, and everything they do.

To be loved by her means to be alive,
to be rooted, to be at home.

ERICH FROMM

Mothers love.
And love.
And love
some more.

My mother is a pretty lady.
I wish to kiss her all day but I have to go to school.

TANIA PRICE, AGE 6, AUSTRALIA

Mothers shine.

Mothers

change a lot of dirty diapers.

Grandmothers

change a few more.

No one but doctors and mothers know
what it means to have interruptions.

KARL A. MENNINGER

Mothers tend,
day and night.

In the eyes of its mother every beetle is a gazelle.

MOROCCAN PROVERB

Mothers
see us
at our
best (and brag
about it).

The sleeping mother and babe hushed,
I study them long and long.

WALT WHITMAN

Mothers
cuddle
better than
anyone.

For children is there any happiness which is not also noise?

FREDERICK W. FABER

Mothers
listen —
at any decibel.

If there were no schools to take the children away
from home part of the time, the insane asylums
would be filled with mothers.

E.W. HOWE

Mothers deserve some time off.

Somehow even her clothes feel different to her children's hands from anybody else's clothes. Only to touch her skirt or her sleeve makes a troubled child feel better.

KATHARINE BUTLER HATHAWAY

Mothers
give us
total
peace
of mind.

To give quickly is a great virtue.

HINDU PROVERB

Mothers know what we need before we know it ourselves.

The patience of a mother might be likened to a
tube of toothpaste—it's never quite all gone.

UNKNOWN

Mothers squeeze us, and we squeeze 'em right back.

He who gives to me teaches me to give.

DANISH PROVERB

Mothers reach out to help those in need.

My mother had a great deal of trouble with me,
but I think she enjoyed it.

Mothers
shake
their heads
and laugh.

Always end the name of your child with a vowel,
so that when you yell the name will carry.

BILL COSBY

Mothers are keeping an eye on you.

Mother love is the fuel that enables a
normal human being to do the impossible.

MARION C. GARRETTY

Mothers *inspire* our greatest achievements.

If evolution really works, how come
mothers only have two hands?

MILTON BERLE

Mothers multitask.

In search of my mother's garden, I found my own.

ALICE WALKER

Mothers
plant
the seed.

Mother's love is peace. It need not be acquired,
it need not be deserved.

ERICH FROMM

Mothers see us at our worst

(and love us all the same).

With bandaids, with wishes, with stories, with kisses—

Mothers heal our hearts.

My mother wanted us to understand that the tragedies of your life one day have the potential to be comic stories the next.

NORA EPHRON

Mothers
tell tales.

Mothers . . . carry the key of our souls in their bosoms.

OLIVER WENDELL HOLMES

Mothers
watch
over us.

"Sit up straight!"
"Pick up your socks!"
"Get a haircut!"
"Do you want to see the cutest baby photos ever?"

Mothers can be
irritating.

Patching your favorite jeans,
breakfast for dinner,
birthday surprises.

Mothers
improvise
(and make it fun).

God couldn't be everywhere, so he created mothers.

JEWISH PROVERB

Mothers protect.

There are times when parenthood
            seems nothing more than feeding
the hand that bites you.

PETER DE VRIES

Mothers keep on cooking.

Variety is the mother of Enjoyment.

BENJAMIN DISRAELI

Mothers make
the simplest things
a whole lot of fun.

We live to play: that is my slogan,
under which we shall set about
the real things in life.

J.B. YEATS

Mothers make
silly faces.

Trust yourself. You know more than you think you do.

BENJAMIN SPOCK

Mothers just may know more than you think.

There is only one happiness in life, to love and be loved.

GEORGE SAND

Mothers give us the greatest joy.

Yes, Mother. I can see you are flawed.
You have not hidden it.
That is your greatest gift to me.

ALICE WALKER

Mothers make mistakes.

A mother never realizes that her
children are no longer children.

HOLBROOK JACKSON

Mothers baby us.

The people who play are the creators.

HOLBROOK JACKSON

Mothers tickle, mothers giggle.

She's always there when you need her.

Mothers lend us a hand, or a buck (or both).

"Splashing in puddles?"

"Finger paints?"

"Mud pies?"

"YES! Then straight to the bubble bath."

Mothers
are happy
to clean up
the mess.

Human beings are the only creatures
on earth that allow their children
to come back home.

BILL COSBY

Mothers
kick us out
of the nest
(but remind us the
door is always open).

"I'll do it by MYSELF!"
"Ugh, Mom you're so annoying!"
"Leave me alone! I HATE you!"

Mothers
take it
in stride.

The successful mother sets her children free and becomes more free herself in the process.

ROBERT J. HAVINGHURST

Mothers
give us
the world.

First published in 2007 by Conari Press,
an imprint of Red Wheel/Weiser, LLC
With offices at:
500 Third Street, Suite 230
San Francisco, CA 94107
www.redwheelweiser.com

ISBN-10: 1–57324–304–3
ISBN-13: 978–1–57324–304–9

Library of Congress Cataloging-in-Publication Data

Mother is a verb / [compiled by] Mina Parker.
 p. cm.
 ISBN 1-57324-304-3 (alk. paper)
 1. Mothers–Quotations. 2. Motherhood–Quotations, maxims, etc. 3.
Mothers–Miscellanea. 4. Motherhood–Miscellanea. I. Parker, Mina.
 PN6084.M6M635 2007
 306.874'3–dc22
 2006021655

Cover and text design by Kristine Brogno
Typeset in Handsome and Gill Sans
Cover and interior illustrations by Kristine Brogno

Printed in Hong Kong
SS

10 9 8 7 6 5 4 3 2 1

an eye on * protect * nurse * tend * forgive * care for * give

play * irritate us * weave stories * can relate * hug and kiss

giggle * wash behind our ears * give us the world * forgive

count to ten * teach * hug and kiss * protect * weave storie

oud * know what's best * tickle and giggle * welcome us hom

an eye on * protect * nurse * tend * forgive * care for * love

play * irritate us * weave stories * can relate * hug and kiss

giggle * wash behind our ears * give us the world * forgiv

count to ten * teach * hug and kiss * protect * weave storie

oud * know what's best * tickle and giggle * welcome us hom

an eye on * protect * nurse * tend * forgive * care for * giv

play * irritate us * weave stories * can relate * hug and kiss

giggle * wash behind our ears * give us the world * forgiv

count to ten * teach * hug and kiss * protect * weave storie

oud * know what's best * tickle and giggle * welcome us hom

an eye on * protect * nurse * tend * forgive * care for * giv

are for * cultivate * attend to * watch over * look after * keep
love * heal * get tough * get all mushy * reach out * inspire
embarrass * give us peace of mind * lend us a hand * make
heal * kick us out * tickle * bathe * welcome us home * listen
deserve the best * scold * feed * give us the world * make us p
are for * cultivate * attend to * watch over * look after * keep
love * heal * get tough * get all mushy * reach out * inspire
embarrass * give us peace of mind * lend us a hand * make
heal * kick us out * tickle * bathe * welcome us home * listen
deserve the best * scold * feed * give us the world * make us p
are for * cultivate * attend to * watch over * look after * keep
love * heal * get tough * get all mushy * reach out * inspire
embarrass * give us peace of mind * lend us a hand * make
heal * kick us out * tickle * bathe * welcome us home * listen
deserve the best * scold * feed * give us the world * make us p
are for * cultivate * attend to * watch over * look after * keep